WITH THIS BODY

WITH THIS BODY

POEMS

Luray Gross

RAGGED SKY PRESS   *Princeton, New Jersey*

Published by Ragged Sky Press

270 Griggs Drive

Princeton, NJ 08540

raggedsky.com

ISBN: 978-1-933974-56-9

Library of Congress Control Number: 2023941417

This book has been composed in Adobe Garamond Pro and Scala

Author photo: Michael M. Koehler

Text and cover design by Pamela L. Schnitter

Cover art: *The Spirit of the Beehive* (detail), Jean Foos and Stephen Talasnik, 2022, acrylic paint on bamboo reed. Photo by Dirk Rowntree.

Printed on acid-free paper. ∞

Printed in the United States of America

For all who have lost a child

Contents

PROLOGUE

SISTER INVICTUS SINGS THE BLUES

So cold and damp this morning,
    the moon forget to shine.
So cold and damp this morning,
    the moon forget to shine.
I left my warm bed,
    left it all behind.

Couldn't sleep this morning
    even though I'm tired.
Can't sleep no more this morning
    even though I'm tired.
Two more hours till sunrise
    but my mind's on fire.

I lost my religion
    in a dream last night.
Lost my sweet religion
    in a dream last night.
Now I'm on my own
    like a string-cut kite.

Will the March wind take me,
    carry me away?
Will the cold wind take me
    carry me away?

Gonna find my own life
    after fifty years delay.

Oh, the kite is sailing
    sailing high above.
Oh, the kite is sailing
    sailing high above
Looking for its own place
    just like Noah's dove.

WITH THIS BODY

for JC

With this body I meet your body.
With your body you meet my body.

Beyond each,
reach of wave and quantum,
canyon rift, cliff.

Apart from other,
body grieves.

Remembered words
do not suffice.

Yet let us speak.
Let our words press
their charges, rattle the heart

Death, wait a while longer.
There is so much to do.

FROM THE WRIST

Goodbyes…
should have their own
place to come from, the elbow
perhaps . . .
　　　　—JILLIAN WEISE

Wrist says, Look.
See what I carry:
bangle, cuff, that
call-for-help scar.

Watch me bend. See me
flick my flag of truce.
Touch me.

Twist of the wrist.
Home of the pulse,
I see you quicken.
I read your teacup hold,
your skipping-stone snap.

Let us be: you/me, me/you,
skin to skin.
We are the breakable ones.
The ones who risk.

THE GRANARY

The barn rose above her, a temple
and she the only worshipper.
Outside, the hot slap of August, but there

in the almost dark, the kernels of wheat
were water she let fall through her fingers,
silk she sifted with bare toes.

No, it was a cavern. She, the only one to venture.
She thrust both arms deep into the grain
and listened for her own breathing.

She must have been close to the rightness
a man feels when his cock rests deep
inside a woman's body.

In bed at night, fist pressed against pubis,
she could bring on those waves,
a pleasure she'd discovered all for herself.

Child, child, under the faded star-pattern quilt,
drunken with loneliness,
already aching with need.

LITTLE GODDESS

after Sharon Olds' "Ode to the Clitoris"

Little Goddess,
how often have you, like any deity,
been offended?
The door you keep
opened with no greeting,
not even a casual touch.

I've not spoken up for you,
rarely said a word on your behalf,
though I discovered you
before I knew who you were.
Lonely child, I could not have guessed,

but you became my comfort,
dependably there in secret
waiting for the pressure of my fist.
You were my lullaby, my quiet
in that place of work and words.

Wellspring, soft key,
little mollusk without a shell.
How could the pleasure
you and I made together
be anything but good?

IN THE ABSENCE OF SUNLIGHT

This body, like tree branches at night, keeps moving—
legs bend, the right knee meeting the left
it has knocked into so many times,

each knock an inquiry: "Are you still with me?
What mischief will we engender together?"
And my right arm tucks itself under torso,
hand lightly fisting belly, pubis.

This body, keeping all its waters of life flowing:
the heart, receiving, releasing, blue turned red,
while the lungs empty and fill, while cilia filter the night-cool air
which is not stopping its own work of moving,

while the mind travels on roads I've never noticed,
though perhaps they were there all the time,
anterooms where work-a-day implements are stored,
where refugee dreams shelter, where all who enter can be fed.

This body, working without my knowledge,
not requiring my consent or the admiration of others,
not even praise from the body sleeping next to me
doing its own work to carry on.

SOMEONE TIED YOUR TINY SHOES

Everything else you have to imagine for yourself. . .
—LAURA KASISCHKE

Yes. They tied them, over and over again,
after the warm bath, after the nap,
after your curious fingers pulled the laces free.
Decades before velcro and several years
before they bought you patent leathers with
shiny metal buckles.

Someone lifted you from the prison of the playpen
and slotted your legs into the highchair, into the swing.
Someone spooned spinach puree into your fish-mouth
and someone pinned a fresh diaper over your bottom.
Someone sang you to sleep, surely, someone must have.

Someone had dreamed you into being
while cows with swollen udders waited in the barn
and bales piled in the haymow held the perfume
of mid-summer and burlap bags in the feed alley
waited for someone to lift each one, balance its weight
on the edge of the cart, pull the string that would
unleash the grain, a cascade of sweetness to be fed
scoop by patient scoop.

The tiny shoes were white,
easily scuffed and marred, but brought back

with a coat of chalky liquid, then let to dry,
and softly polished.
The leather was soft as your toddler cheeks,
soft as your mother's belly.

The next child, already in her womb,
was busy hatching a plan
to be the one who would have tantrums
while you pouted and willed her to stop.

Someone tied your shoes. Someone brushed your hair.
Did they imagine you now, after so many years, so many shoes,
so many ties of blood and affection kept and broken?

"IT KEPT COMING BACK TO MY MOUTH"

for Patricia Smith, whose poem gave me the title

Bean, bean. String bean.
Words I put into summer air,
their sound separate from dinner, kitchen, plate.
Not pick, sort, snap, chew or swallow.
Not seed and plant, not grow and green.
Bean was just a shape in my mouth.

I was seven? I was eight? I was not
an age, but a mind and word cut off
from meaning, repeating
its march: One, Two, One.
String. Bean. String. Bean.
Left, right, left.

Before that afternoon, words
had been the things themselves.
My name was me, as sky was the blue beyond.
How odd then, when suddenly,
a sound could mean any thing at all.

Might sweep or blaze, might weep or shout.
Could have been switched in the cradle or cave
in time that stretched endlessly backward.
Bean for clock or barn. *Bean* for table, mother, bread.

How perilous and shifting the word/the world
had become: something made by chance.
Each thing could have been other.
I could have been another child
in another family, in another house.

What I knew for sure was like the flecks of dust
that never came to rest on my outstretched palm.

SCAB

When I was a child as any other child,
I picked my scabs, eagerly sliding a fingernail
under dark crumbly edges, along the healing shine,
then tugged the last bits free
to watch fresh red lift to the surface
at the center of each scrape and cut.

How I loved the taste of blood, the taste of truth,
my own private consolation as I sat
in the little chair pulled back
from the edge of my desk
where the reader lay open to "Look" or "Run."
By the next day, a new scab would form,
smaller but still enough to satisfy.

I want to sit next to that girl now.
Perhaps she will, like Emma yesterday,
rise from her seat and proclaim her luminous poem,
though I suspect, even after all these years,
all she will summon will be a whisper,
a voice I barely remember, one I drown out
when I put on my raven mask,
my adornments of confidence and authority.

Each April, the tree below our window
turns to fragrant blossom for a week—
dependable loveliness, which just as dependably

scatters over the ragged lawn.
By July, the leaves mottle with scab and canker.
By August, the tree is bare.
Each summer we consider taking it down.

I used to assume I saved the tree for its beauty,
not its months of leafless blight,
another way I have been mistaken.

POEM IN FLANNEL PAJAMAS

After her grandmother died, and the room was hers,
she pushed the bed against the windowsill.
Winter ferned the panes, the moon
traversed the fields.

Moon on her left, if she lay on her back;
on her right, when her belly pressed the sheets.
The night the owl called her awake,
she sat to see its bulk upon the limb,

a silhouette that leaned into each call.
Not robin, grackle, sparrow, dove
that daily dipped in the birdbath below.
She felt it then. She owned those depths.

Darkness dwelt inside her.
Not just the bird's talon,
its looming eye,
its treacherous beak.

YOUR MOTHER'S HIP

Never again will I ride on her hip
or shelter in the keep of her belly.
Neither do I remember.
I felt the weight and cling of my own child
on my own hip, the left,
to keep my right arm free for all the doing.

I remember the solidity of my belly
as each child grew and tumbled,
an aquanaut in deep warm dark.
I remember the ripple of the swimmer's
kick and the soft fontanel of the newborn.

I remember my own hand tapping—
no slapping—the crown of a three-year-old's head
in a slip, an impulse, a failure,
and the child's question, "Why did you do that?"

The chair in your poem, Samira,
is overturned, and perhaps, only perhaps,
righted again. If so, by what force,
with what intent and for what duration?

Each of us is overturned and tumbled,
bowled over, undone . . . .
There are blues we only hum,
having never learned the words.
The melody goes through its changes without them,
sinks below middle C, then quickens and rises.

We ride that horse, ungentled, unreined,
from motherland through the valley of shadows
and out again, our fingers closed around
handfuls of mane, our knees clutched tight,
chins lifted, mouths open, drinking the wind.

A SMALL FACT

is that my mother was a twin.
She mentioned that only once,
telling me—though sometimes I think

I imagined that confidence—the other fetus
did not develop, was expelled
when she was born, and I think

that must be why always
under her wit, her gaiety, her resolve,
lived a sadness so deep she herself

could not christen it with a name,
could not grasp that phantom
that made her keep her secrets close

as though there was only one
who might know what they were.
Not even our father, whom, it seemed

she loved and to whom she spoke
of things she would not tell
her daughters, not wanting

to burden us when already
we were fetching cows and feeding calves,
or making supper and taking care of each other

all before sitting at the long table
in the dining room to do our homework
to bring home the As and our teachers' praise.

Or was it because she herself could not
bear to bare herself before us,
we who lifted our faces to hers.

OF   OF   THE
WITH LINES FROM SAPPHO

only fragments   ~~have been found~~

It's no use

Mother dear, I tell you now

                    I *wore a soldier's*
                      cloak dyed purple
                        (no matter it resembled a dress)

                    Say what you please
                      Say what,
                            what you please
                                    I will not hear you

                                    Blindness
                    is much stronger
                    than a man's heart
                        (Oh, but a woman's . . .)

                                        in meadows
                                      where horses
                                          have grown sleek
                                      among spring flowers

Although they are   bloodroot
                                           rue anemone

only breath
                         toothwort
                                 saxifrage

We know this much
         Death is an evil   You are *dust*

                                                       wind-carried,
                                                        far from home

                              I hold what remains—
                                    these curls of soft hair.

                                    your beautiful, boisterous hair

MILK AND HONEY

She's all curves and folds, black spandex
from the shoulders of her halter top
to the cuffs of her capris,
quick-stepping along the path,
cell pressed to ear.

I'm running by with my skinny legs
and my skinny dog
on his teflon-coated leash,

and I could be thinking
of her extra pounds
or why, oh why
must she gossip here,

but I'm thinking:
milk and honey, milk and honey,
oh, Goddess,
let your hair hang down.

TONGUE

Tongue flicks, lizard quick,
to spear and spar.

Tongue that lashes, sneers,
likes having teeth so near.

That weary tongue, tending words
the mind can barely reach.

Tongue that seeks
the cock's hot root

or circumnavigates the breast
and tugs the nipple's firm dark tip.

Tongue to tongue,
that urgent tussle.

Lasso me, wrangler tongue.
Urge me in.

II

A BULLET WITH YOUR NAME ON IT

Las Vegas, October 1, 2017

Capable, ready to speed toward you
  Heather, Austin, Charleston, Rhonda, Bill
Not that you were hiding. You didn't know
the game was being played
  Neysa, Adrian, Kurt, Jenny, Brian
You heard music, then the errant sound
of firecrackers in the crowd,
until you couldn't stand or cry out
  Christopher, Thomas, Jack, Jordyn, Carrie
Under some of you the living hid;
some skidded on your blood, still vivid
  Cameron, Lisa, Brett, Victor, Angela
Most of us who read your names know nothing
of who you were or who you left behind
  Quinton, Hannah, Denise, Bailey, Chris
Someone stood at a hotel window
armed with the forward motion of his plans
  Melissa, Laura, Erick, Austin, Nicol
He did not know you
  Jennifer, Rachael, Rocio, Christiana, Michelle
Who else must bear the guilt?
  Sandy, Keri, Lisa, Kelsey, Tara, Candace
We who were not there, who never met
the man who had so many fooled?
  Steve, Denise, Stacee, Dana, John

You were in the frame
>*Laura, Calla, Susan, Andrea, Carly*
>*Dorene, James, Patricia, Carolyn, Derrick*
>*Jessica, Brennan*

You were in the frame
and we were not

GOD DOES WHAT SHE WANTS

God does what she wants. She has very large
Tractors.
——ROBERT BLY

Busy with those tractors,
God doesn't have time to care,
doesn't seem to mind if a 38-year-old mother
shoots both of her sons in their beds.

God is busy
driving her newest tractor
while their bodies, artificially functioning,
are transported to a hospital where,
once the proper papers are signed,
organs will be harvested, tissue harvested,
retinas harvested, skin kept supple for grafting.

God's hungry tires churn
whether or not the mother,
a thousand dollars in arrears for her rent,
has or has not been apprehended
while the boys' classmates gather
in a sanctuary where a pastor tells them,
You should not have to bear this,
not at your age.

Not at any age should a child
rub the blood of a classmate

over her own wounded body
so the boy with the rifle will think
she too is already dead.

Not at any age, we say, should a person
need to stumble over the bodies
of those who cannot flee
in order to try to save herself.

Who mourns with the spring grasses?
Who weeps with the river of rain?
How can we bear to hear those tractors grinding?

SUNDAY MORNING IN MY NEARLY
ALL-WHITE NEIGHBORHOOD

I

5:00 a.m. Moon at apogee flanked by Mars.
Venus and Aldebaran, eye of the Bull,
rising in the east.

I walk three miles, encounter nineteen deer,
a fox that utters two brief cries, then lopes away,
a robin with a curious white-collar mutation.
Two prosperous minivans, one pickup,
one skinny runner wearing headphones.
No one else out but me

in this "good" neighborhood.
The earnest man next door
tells me, *I'm not racist.*
I'm not even white, look, I'm tan.
"We all bleed RED," the sign
in his front lawn proclaims. He's trying.

II

And I? Raised on 116 acres my ancestors
turned and tilled, doing work
envisioned by 20 black preachers
who met with General Sherman on January 12, 1865,
and told him, Give us land and leave us alone.

You can read the history: how four days later,
Sherman issued Special Field Order Number 15,
setting aside over 400,000 acres
from Charleston south to the St. John's.

How by June, 40,000 "freedmen" had settled on "Sherman's Land;"
how before the year was out, Andrew Johnson overturned the order.
How that broken promise has spiraled through our history,
history most of us do not acknowledge,

us being those with skin like mine, pale and freckled,
something I sometimes think I would not choose.
My white skin and how it ushers
me through the world, even now
when I tap out these words.

ON THE DAY OF THE FIRST MEMORIAL
SERVICE FOR GEORGE FLOYD

I've come in from the deck for some distance
from a row between our neighbor and his girlfriend.
I've learned more about both of them
than I need to know,

but I'm not their concern, any more than I
was what harried the woman
who raged under the bridge this afternoon.
She sat among rocks. It's been such a dry spring.

Her son, maybe 17, leaned his bike against the rail,
talked her back onto our barely-traveled road.
Arms scissoring, mouth still going,
she marched away as he got back on the bike.

It took only a minute for him to tell me,
"We're the closest a mother and son can be.
I've never seen her like this."

What was his name? Would his mother come to harm?
I imagine again Rilke's bowl of roses—
the white, the yellow, the pink—
how his poem says they
would make you forget the hatred
balled in two boys' fighting fists;

though, of course, since those boys
are there in the first stanza,
we know the poet remembered.

We say we will never forget.
We say it and we do forget, or we blur memory,
turn laceration to scrape, turn bullet to slap,
We put a tensed hand back in a pocket.
What does it see?

Even there it is not guiltless.

A MAP OF YOUR VILLAGE

When Li Jinwei was four years old, a neighbor abducted him.
Three decades later, calling only on memory,
he drew a map of his home village
and posted it on a video-sharing app.
Now he has been reunited with his mother.
You can see their tears, hear their cries.

If it had been Melanie Bieler, rather than Li Jingwei,
could she have drawn a map of her small town, true enough
to be recognized by a stranger idling away an afternoon?
Would she remember the oil-stained concrete, the Texaco star?

Bieler's garage is gone, its bricks tumbled, soil scraped,
gas pumps scrapped. Chuck Bieler himself, safely in his grave.
His spoiled daughter must be in her eighth decade.
The golf course he named after her has sprouted luxury
     townhouses.

I barely remember Melanie herself, but I could draw
her main street, with Stauffer's Store—post office included—
and Blackie's Barbershop, where one afternoon our father,
fed up with our complaining, took both me and my sister,
directed Blackie to chop off our braids.

For decades I thought nothing of the barber's nickname,
Peter Black being a short white man, white as nearly everyone

in that town. We didn't know we were waiting for the earth to shift.
Waiting for a new story to be told.

When Li Jingwei returned to his village, touched again
the face of his mother, what was stranger: that she knew him,
that he knew her? That both of them had been wounded, or
that both of them began to heal?

ON ASSIGNMENT AT THE HOME FOR DISTURBED CHILDREN: POLAND, 1948

Chim picked up his camera the way a doctor takes his
stethoscope out of his bag.
—HENRI CARTIER-BRESSON

He came to Tereska,
to the place she had been taken
after the liberation,
after the camps.

Chim came
with his camera—
witness, diagnostician.

Someone dressed her in sturdy wool.
Someone starched her white collar.
Someone pinned an over-sized bow in her hair.
Someone led her to the blackboard and said,
"Draw home."

She drew a tangle of lines,
a nest of wire. She drew journey
without destination.

Someone called her name,
or dropped a pen, or coughed,
and she turned,
still holding the chalk in her hand,

and Chim opened the shutter

just long enough
to show us her naked face,
her piercing gaze.

ELLIPSIS

Our daughter has not remembered her dreams
for months. Her husband has gained all of the freight
his father shed.

A child in the woods takes a stick to his eye.
The surgeon operates: stitches and secures
what has been severed.

We want their lives not to be fraught,
perhaps to be happy.

For them, we want that space in which nothing
needs, nothing wants, nothing urges,
nothing speaks.

God of emptiness, let them float unmoored.
Let the sea be calmed. Let the opening
to the harbor be near.

THE SKY

for Tyree and Tyyon Bates, Philadelphia, PA, July 18, 2018

I

For two years John Constable painted clouds, only clouds.
The sky, he wrote a friend, is the chief organ of sentiment.
If its notes could be heard, all else might follow.

Today, clouds shift and gather. They thin, then aggregate—
their notes too low or high for the human ear.
We know thunder, its basso proclamations,
its rumble growl. We know the keening of wind.

"I know he's coming back,"
the brother of the gunned-down 14-year-old says.
"Is that like a dream?" Until now, only a year separated them,
one year and three letters in their names.

So much we do not know: how to mend what is broken,
how to claim what has been healed,
how to rightly apologize, how to do a needful thing.

II

How *is* one to live? We come back to the question,
jolted and consoled by sky or sea or the depth of an eye,
the strident power of bow on strings,
of hammers hitting the keys.
Constable painted. Some of us just yearn.

Yesterday began in coral and gold. Pink/gray clouds flocked
circumference of sky. What notes the dawn was offering
I will never know complete, though I tried to listen.
Love, St. Paul wrote, *beyond all, love.*

Kubler-Ross sat by a dying girl and watched her draw a tank.
In front of it, a stick figure holding a sign that said STOP.
The doctor took the pencil and did all she could:
she drew another person steadying that child.

I spend hours looking at an immensity of sky:
troposphere . . . mesosphere . . .exosphere . . .
Sometimes it is too difficult to look down.
Impossible, it seems, to hold that child's hand.

BLUEBEARD'S BOOTS

We chew on the seem and divide
of our lives, turning gruel
to muscle, muscle to gruel.

Forgetfulness opens its mouth,
its tongue, a long tingling drawbridge,
and swallows us.

Bluebeard's boots echo up and down.
In his dwelling there is ample room
for one more bride,

ignorant and charmed,
ready to slide into his car
and ride off into the night,

the dashboard alive
and he much younger-seeming
than possible.

FROM THE CAVE

Each morning I listen to their stories:
Every two seconds, a girl is forced or given
into marriage. Perhaps she is 10 years old,
perhaps 12. She may have been seized from school
or from the path down to the river and
sold, bartered, raped, starved, or burned.
She was loved by a mother
who could not change her fate.

While I enter the space of the page freely,
Suliman says, "They treated me like a drug dealer,
pulled us out of our seats before the plane
taxied down the runway."
Halma says she did not sleep all last night.
Though she and her children made it
to Massachusetts a week ago,
will her sister's family be barred?

K. is not sure he will be able to return to New York
where he has lived for twelve years,
but adds, "I continue to believe
that making music is an act of freedom."
So he plays, he sings, he dreams.

This is what I have to tell you:
The bowl is broken, the bread dipped
in kerosene and set afire.

We who are bathed in excess
light our way by its sooty flame
as though nothing, nothing will stop us.

A FEW NOTES FROM THE ANTHROPOCENE

We painted mammoths and bears, horses and bulls
    left handprints deep in the heart of the cave

Invented alphabets, inscriptions
    mastered brush, pen, and sword

We brewed mead with bees' honey
    wine with sun-swollen grapes

Grew barley and spelt, quinoa and wheat
    flooded plains to plant rice

Gathered persimmons, the bitter and sweet
    plucked juniper berries to flavor our drink

Bred cattle and horses
    hitched oxen to sledges and plows

Powered wheel, crankshaft, and lever
    hammer, piston, gear

Stood on assembly lines and breadlines
    staked out the line in the sand

We harvested lemons and pomegranates
    pineapples, mangoes, and guava

Traded cinnamon, ginger, cardamom
    pepper and cloves, tulip bulbs
    mast pines, diamonds, and coal

We cut reeds for panpipes and flutes
    fashioned guitars and capos
    fiddles with elegant bows

Wove damask and linen, denim
    wool, cotton, and silk

Minted pennies and rubles
    pesos, cordobas, and yen

Built highways, runways and piers
    rockets, boosters, and bombs

Turned mold into cures, stitched sutures
    ground lenses, read x-rays and 3-D scans

We brought law, we brought order
    infraction and crime

We believed in exclusion, fenced the borders
    and barred the gates

We brought discord and fracture, union and healing
    We prospered. We blundered.
    We multiplied.

ANOTHER LETTER TO NÂZIM

I stepped out of my thoughts of death
and put on the June leaves of the boulevards.
—NÂZIM HIKMET

Early spring here, Nâzim, but I'm going to follow you
and put the June leaves of the boulevards
on my wrists, my shoulders, the crown of my head.
Nâzim, I'll be once more what now I barely remember.

This afternoon, I'm stepping back
from the numbers of cases and deaths,
back to the ten-thousand-line poem
you decided to write in prison,
a poem of the people of your country.

I'm imagining you reading your lines to other prisoners,
the most informed critics, who could tell you,
Yes, this is Anatolia; or No, he never would say that;
she would never…

Nâzim, I'm picturing you later, in exile,
sitting among friends at that table in Moscow
in March of the year your heart would fail, gazing
at a cucumber "pebbly and fresh as a daisy."

Here, daisies have begun to dot the field
below my asparagus patch, lording it briefly

over the oncoming stilt grass.
Tangible specters of virus,
foolhardiness and fear surround us,
but my right foot has pierced the barrier.
My left is already in motion.
I'm coming, though my body remains here in my kitchen.

Wait for me at the next corner.
Lean against the signpost and whistle till I slip my arm in yours.
We'll stroll beneath the lindens, investigate the oaks,
note plum blossoms shriveled on the pavement,
still holding their pink.

We'll buy warm bread glazed with butter.
We'll watch swallows thread the noon-blue sky.
Nâzim, not even your cell or our inevitable deaths
will stop us.

THE FOOL NAMED HOPE

*Most of the time I like to take my seat next to the fool
named Hope.*
> —ALICIA OSTRIKER

I

I was a tiny thing with feathers,
a bafflement to my parents
who took me home and reared me
just like Stuart Little, with no cage, no bars.
My mother breathed
sweetness into my breast.
My father held out his palm
and let me rest there.
I was a wonder, a query, a quandary—
yet they fed me, clothed me.
Let me fly.

II

Some say I was the one thing left in that stone jar
Pandora could not help but open,
but no one knows if my presence there
was curse or blessing.

III

Our friend was already leaving
when she walked into the gun shop,
another friend told me.

How sure her plans,
how evident her resolve.

IV

It seems no family is exempt—
none without a brother, a niece,
a neighbor, a workmate—
someone left with only their wreckage.

I want a simple answer,
a slipknot yielding to a tug.
Some part of me wants
to be a child
running my fingers
through a fern's soft frills,
finding refuge.

V

As though it weighs too much to carry,
I keep setting Hope down, ready to desert
that simpleton hardly anyone expects
to have a future. Then I hear its faint squall
and take that child back
into my arms.

POEM BEGINNING WITH A LINE FROM GREGORY ORR

The reader is the lover, the text the beloved,
though, of course, the beloved
becomes lover soon or late.

The blackbird sings to the marsh
and the marsh plays its grasses,
its slowly moving waters.

Thirteen, I carried the library book home
and hid in a place where only I
would receive the text's sly glances.

I was the one the words had been waiting for
no matter how many names had been scribbled
on the card in the sleeve inside the cover.

I added my own—the name of its one true love.

TO TOUCH LANGUAGE

I'm trying to touch language via the page once a day.
—DANEZ SMITH

I am trying to touch the silence
of words, to run my fingers
over their faint Braille.

Trying to summon the courage
of the blind man with no arms
who read texts with his lips
as we read each others' in a kiss.

A child, I hid his photograph
in a dresser drawer lest by seeing,
I might myself be disarmed.

Now I touch language like that child
tracing the letters of her name,
her very self placed there
in stark lines and curves,

caved and canyoned, carried
between the urge and the stay,
the impulse and the leash.

I'm trying to feel light within words,
not just in the spaces between them.

I'm trying to believe language
can be suture, quilt, meteor,
parachute.

THE SHAPE OF USEFULNESS

I try to fit language into the shape of usefulness.
—CLAUDIA RANKINE

The shape of a salt crystal, for example,
or a needle, a wedge, a bolt.
I try to fit language into the curve
of a chalice or cupped hand,
or the flat dry rock just big enough
to step on before you leap to the far bank.

Fit language into the waterwheel's turning
or the piston's thrust. Into the shape of an ember
holding heat enough to be urged back into flame.
Sometimes, into the shape of a kiss.

I try to fit language into the breath
of a sigh or a frantic wave.
Into raindrop, dewdrop, teardrops.
I press words between pages of a heavy book
and wait months for them to speak.

They could be blade or arrow, basket or bowl,
rope or ladder, chisel or hammer,
but I want my words to be fabric anyone can shape
into shirt or shroud, altar cloth, bandage, or banner.

Tell me where you are wounded.
Tell me what you need.

PLACE UNKNOWN/KNOWN

I wish I knew the chamber of the mind,
its deepest caverns, its Chapel of Lions,
its Galerie du Fond, but I've rarely gone
beyond the prehistoric entrance,
never shimmied on my belly

in the dark and mud to press
through the Crawling Passage.
Instead I read of those
amazed by the curled bison
on the ceiling of Altamira—

its ochre hue, its looming power,
the aurochs in the Hall of Bulls
in Lascaux. That's what I'm going
to do today, after I lower the lid
of this laptop. I'll travel to France

on wings of words, unworried
about what I might find were I
to close my eyes and let my
monkey mind hold sway. If I were
to follow each strand of thought,

leap with it across canyons,
not fearing in the least the raging
stream below, would I know any more

about that gray and seemingly
undefined mass of nerve and charge?

Perhaps never, but tonight
I'll enter the dreamworld
with a guide as eloquent as Virgil,
and be schooled again by seeing, feeling,
what I cannot know by day.

POEM WITH THE TEENSY TATTOO

The poem with the teensy tattoo
you'll never get to see talks big
but keeps her private matters
private.

She wasn't made for consumption
or market value. All her riches
grew in the dark. Her own joy,
her own sadness, sufficient light and heat.

She let her pigtails jounce
as she skipped rope
in a corner of the playground.
Bent over her library book,
she felt them fall over her shoulders.

What was not given she found
in an empty cicada shell,
a ribbon of spent snakeskin,
one gray feather drifting into her palm.
At school, the teacher's frown leaned over her
and she did not shrink.

Awkward, a bit chunky,
she was the girl-child
who never made the team, never

had a coach's hands pause
as they cruised her bum.

The smallest butterfly
inked on her thigh was still to come.
"Will you go back, or will you
go forward?" the fairies asked.
The butterfly opened its glamorous wings
and flew.

WHAT THE POEM CARRIES

This poem wants to *be* an ant, purposeful
and sure of the path, not alone,
but marching in line carrying a flag
cut out of leaf, a flag larger than its body,
flag of all countries that shouts, *Yes* and *Forward*
and *Together Now.*
This poem wants to blend in a chorus,
sounding any note of the chord.

This poem knows gloom won't get it anywhere fast,
maybe not even slowly, so this poem says, "Yes,
I'm alive and I'm going to wear my vintage hot-pink miniskirt,
a bargain from the consignment shop,
and click the heels of my cowboy boots.
I'm going to laugh till I cry, then
I'm going to drink sweet tea with lemon and extra ice."

This poem shakes your hand or rests its arm on your shoulder,
whispers, "There, there, honey, you go on and cry if you need to."
This poem carries extra kleenex in its purse
and won't mind at all if you make it late for the bus.
This poem will hold out its thumb at the curb

believing in the mercy of strangers
and the necessity of danger.

This poem won't text while you're telling your story
for the seventh time, seven being its lucky number
on days when three and five are taking a break.
This poem knows we all need a break from despair
and all that residual sadness. It's been around long enough
to know that the blues are really love songs
and making peace with terror
is the price you pay to stay alive.

UPON READING NICANOR PARRA'S
ANTIPOEMAS

I'll adjust my bowler hat
and take my black umbrella to the park.
I'll be looking, all the while, for a suitable
branch to hang them from.

It's just the day
for a swim in the nude, for a session diving
with the stop-over loons in their white necklaces,
as out of place here as poodles in puree.

We know Poetry is after all of us,
but we're not afraid, just alert.

This morning's horoscope, the racing digits
on the gas pump, brittle plasticware
at the Discount Dollar Store: all poems.
We can see beyond the labels.

My heart might be empty, but it does have eyes;
eyes and an invisible mouth.

Wry and wretched little mouth, speak
to me, not just to the crowds.

IT WAS JANUARY

It was January and I was heading home
with the memory of a stage kiss in my right back pocket
and the echo of your arms around my shoulders
the last time we danced to the Beatles, slow dance,
if one can really call that small circle you led me in a dance.

It was January and a gray-haired man with an Indian accent
drove his Subaru right through the red light as I entered the
    intersection.
I tried to apply some speed, but knew in a second of smack
    and spin,
I'd not avoided him after all.

After the witness, after the cop, while I waited for the tow,
my mind was on the evening, on how I'd planned to get back
    in my car
and drive south to be there to hear my old friend read
from his new book of poems. We knew this would be his last,
and I had already cautioned myself, touch him gently.

Now all the new-car smell is gone. Soon it will be a year
since he died. I've yet to wear his soft burgundy vest,
the one thing I took from the table at the memorial gathering.

The events of each day keep receding on your Facebook
    Timeline,

yours and mine, but those pickles in the fridge, back near the
    frost line,
they're still the color of envy. The jar still holds the tang of
    regret.
If you look closely, there's always a little something extra.

Yesterday an ant disappeared when it crossed from red to black
on the checkered cloth we'd spread across the table, and in the
    woods
I discovered a rabbit's fur could be all that is left of rabbit
after fox strikes or red-tail barrels down.

I used to think that time was a human invention.
I'd learned about layers and studied road cuts on long rides
    across the state,
but it still came as a surprise to learn there's a clock
in nearly every cell of every living thing.

The Sky Rocket at the fair might have failed inspection, the
    chairs
not firmly fastened to the splintery floor, but the ticket taker
opens and closes the little gate and lets the riders in.

Most mornings, most afternoons, I get in my car and drive.

STONE AT THE BOTTOM OF THE LAKE

Sometimes I think I've lost whole cities,
elaborate constructions in classic Lego red and white.
But perhaps only dresser drawers
like the top one in Aunt Esther's spare bedroom,
smelling of lavender and secret lives.

I stood and looked long into the cloudy mirror
at a girl whose face seemed to show
nothing of what was inside.

I gripped the glass knobs, opened the drawer,
slipped both hands in, then slowly out,
just to touch, not to take.

Now, when I fear speaking the truth,
who do I think is listening?
The stone at the bottom of the lake is wiser than I.

Still, I write, hoping for luck, for the dive
into waking dream or flight beyond
the four-way stop. Jump. Run. Look. Stay.

ESCAPE

Words are my prisons; words my escape:
thou shalt not to *why ever not,*
from playpen to lake floor
where fishes knock on my doors
and I, having no fear, beg them enter.

Words encode strictures,
each with iron spikes to collar
my throat. But I sing in spite,
in spite of the dragon smoke
and the father's sorrow.

I sang my mother's belly as it stretched,
again, again, again. I buttoned the buttons,
snapped the sleeper snaps,
laid the sisters in their cribs
and patted their backs. Then I left them
to hold our father's tears, our mother's
disappointment.

I sat on the floor of my room and opened
the yellow book and read the words aloud.
I let them infuse, I warmed to their simmer.
I followed their glimmer, up and out
through the summer-open window,
through the branches of the silver maple,
out and over the field.

This is how I came into my self,
even though I was barely more than mirage,
a flickering pool leading forward.

When I am no longer body,
no longer ammonia bite of age,
tang of winterberry, will I be
any thing? any where?
I have not escaped the old questions
even though I know the answers, know

the iron in my body will make a three-inch nail
strong enough to secure the box that holds my body.
One you could wrench from its bearing,
and pound into bracelet, ring.

One that would clink in the bucket of your heart
like prayer in the ear of the forgotten god
of justice, the god of equanimity.

Then I will turn into smoke, into cinder,
or recompose myself as humus, loamed
and worm-worked, wholly holy.

PRAYER

The verdant burn,
   a verse of owls.

A mare's tail,
   that wag and swish.

One hundred stallions
   and none to ride.

The knick-knack,
   knock and bewilderment.

The unsayable.

Would-to-god, Candy Man,
   you were here.

You, with your dog-gone
   happy blues.

IV

YOU WOULDN'T WANT TO LIVE FOREVER

but you would want just one more
of those mundane extraordinary dawns.
Then another, another after that,
in spite of melting ice in Greenland
and the persistence of greed.

You'd want another morning
of sex and sweat followed by showers,
dog walks, and coffee. You want
another meatloaf sandwich on soft whole wheat
and another conversation about what it means to be human.

You want deep magenta dahlias as large as dinner plates
and the question your grandson asked,
"Are there any trees just called Tree?"
Only the Tree of Life and the Tree of Love.

You want the persistence of the hammer and the trowel,
the two-note call of the phoebe and the crow's black talk.
You want another chance to wash your face in a cold stream.

You want to be any age at all again—eleven, seventeen, or sixty
when you thought to yourself, *I have forty years left,*
and you speared that banner into the soil. You rallied.

Do you want to live forever? Of course you do.
You want years and years more of wondering,
flicking the reins of *why* with both hands,
urging that horse forward. . .

SEND THE LAZY MAN

Make sure to send a lazy man for the Angel of Death.
—YIDDISH PROVERB

It took the lazy man a full day to get on the road,
and when he finally slid his backside into the driver's seat,
the sun-warmed steering wheel felt so good in his hands,
he leaned his forehead against it and closed his eyes.
The Angel of Death could wait, he thought,
let's give those folks at the bedside a little more time.
But finally he sat up straight, shifted from Park to Drive.

The lazy man supposed he ought to have some explanation
for his tardiness. He found himself rehearsing what he might
    say—
something about a rogue cloud,
a neighbor's lost dog, or a summons delivered
by a surely-no-more-than-nineteen-year-old lackey
of the law. Just wouldn't do to admit his own laziness
was what had taken him so long.

And how, he wondered, was he to bring up the subject
when and if he found that Angel at home.
It's not my idea, but…. If you aren't too busy….?
Miles and miles can unwind
while your let your mind drift.
The lazy man never quite got over that.

He knew the car radio might keep him focused,
but listening to country or even classical or jazz
seemed disrespectful, seeing that he was
about to invite Death into a room.

We don't know whether he made it or not.
Did he get sidetracked at a rest stop or take a detour
that never returned to the main route?
Maybe when he finally arrived,
he couldn't bring himself to knock.

A SMALL GOD

> *A small god*
> *surely lives in my throat*
> *a kind of temple*
> —ELY SHIPLEY

This is a song
for the small god
lodged in my throat,
demanding so little—
no altar, no incense,
not even a secret
unpronounceable name.

With her powers
never fully extinguished
she lives
with the passing winds
of inhale/exhale
and interludes of held breath.

She signals
her godly thought:
Breathe,
and I do,
drawing in the cool air
of morning,
not yet laden with duty.

Beloved by the heart,
the lungs, the electric brain,
she guards my waking and my sleep.
I would praise her,
sing of her beauty,
her trustworthiness.

Small god housed in my throat,
were you there before my birth?
Where will you go when I am gone?

GRAY GRIEF OR BLUE

Last night a friend said,
"I have to stop writing these grief poems."
But even the flashy zinnias speak of mortality,
some after gradual decline, some with swiftness—
the errant pruner, the carelessly bent stem.
Life force cut off so easily.

How many times have you been stunned
by the sheer fact that you are alive?
After all of it, after the rusty nail
piercing the foot, after the crash, the chemo,
the poisonous brew, after dread and disappointment.

Just this morning
you woke to the sound of rain, its steady
simmer, then pour and pound.
It didn't let up for hours;
already browned lawns are pondering green.
Umbrellas, unused for months, walk down
the road with their dogs.

This life, the one you still have,
long ago you learned it wasn't fairly allotted,
or fairly protected by humans
from wind, water, earthquake, and fire.

A child, you dreamed flames licking the window frames
of the house where you were born.
Helpless, you stood in the upstairs hall,
then woke to stillness and dark, the blessed dark,
as dark as your sister's wet hair
in another dream, her hair and her hands,
both beyond reach in the deep.

Fifty years pass, and both of you,
until this moment, survive. Chances are
you will both be alive tomorrow. You will have
more days for grief, gray grief or blue.
Any color will do for weeping.

ROCK

Nothing out of the ordinary,
just the sound of water trickling
over stone and around a plastic bottle
blown out of a recycling pail
or tossed from a truck
or dropped by a heedless runner.

The morning was gray,
but my dogs paused
to read the news, and I noticed
the fine grain of the sandy soil
heavy rains had deposited

and the familiar dark maroon of the rock
in this part of the state where I was born
and where now for twenty years
I have lived again.

Unremarkable, not shining with mica
or coursing with streaks of pink or silver,
not suggesting a history of volcanic spume
or intense heat.

Just the slow attentions of time,
the way it compresses our stories
into something durable,
something that can be broken
yet remain.

A SERIOUS TALK

opening with a line from Valerie Fox

The river invited her down for a serious talk. Not what she
thought. Not tangerine lounge chairs or bedside humble pie.
Not that February robin plucking berries from the holly or
bad news on the radio. Not consolation, not even bedraggled
beauty.

Another river stood by the door in case she grabbed her keys,
attempted a grand auto escape. Those rivers—always in league,
always marching with the ghosts of Romans on a trusty road.

The river who wanted to talk had something on its mind,
always restless confined to its bed. Invalid of the first order.
That river wanted something of her. She had suspected. She
had actually known.

Haven't you known as well? Known the river wanted some-
thing of you, something you claimed you didn't own, hadn't
thieved or purloined, hadn't ever/even borrowed.

You must know how that woman felt. You're still that kid
scuffing your sneakers on the tiles as you head to the principal's
office. That note you'd scribbled and sailed across the rows. The
river has it on her desk.

But the river calls and you go. You're Whitman-armored, Emily-gowned. WCW is in your back pocket. Wallace is walking by your side. All the old guard, in case the less experienced fold.

You choose a tree to lean against and breathe. You listen, trying to unweave the river's syllables, its depth and song.

You hope against lightning, thunder, earthquake, hurricane. You hope for a gust out of the west, blowing all those settlers back into the ocean. You'll ride on its currents. You know how to swim.

River, you shout, I'm one of yours. Let's have it.

ROPE OF STAR

This is a rope of star tied to my wrist.
—CHARLES WRIGHT

Look closer:
light strained through atmosphere,
interstellar until now,
circling my wrist
in place of watch or bangle,
hospital ID band
or cuff hammered from iron

or one of linen, crisply starched
or the loop of a leash
or a lock of love's long hair
or seaweed, dripping, rich with salt,
or the tug of a promise
or the drapery of mourning.

There is a rope of star
tied to my wrist
even when I deny it.
There it is, reading my pulse,
counting my strides,
linking me to a source long dead,
inscribed without alphabet,
woven on a loom of light.

Take my hand.
I'll slip this strand over my palm,
my knuckles, my fingertips
and slide it onto yours.
Then you will shine,
incandescent,
—yes, I will say it—
beautiful.

REJECTING ELEGANCE

I

Elegance resides
in the minute world
of mosses

on stone, trunk,
bark, brick, concrete,

solving nothing.

II

Eight days ago,
the child

was
a splash of life

filled each space

was.

III
Now, a crater
sorrow tries to fill

dipping hands deep
into the soft earth

beneath rain-melted,
freeze-hardened
grayed and cindered
snow of late February.

IV
Give us
inelegance—

mischief mayhem,
push/pull/pummel
rock/roll/run

shout.

V
The child singing
until the tune
is lost,

turned inside out
upside-downed,

the words,
a jumble.

The child,
headstrong
whole, unheeding
heartstrong,

holy here.

SIX WHITE ROSES

Not one
on the cusp of opening
will banish
grief and blame,

yet
mother, aunt,
cousin, father
reach out.

Each
touches the petals
with a fingertip
or a gaze

before looking
away
and beyond
to the future
without the child.

PEONIES IN JULY

Sometimes memory does suffice,
but today I want peonies
in May-time fullness, bending
their weight, their explosions of joy.

I want to bury my hands
in their cool white plush,
run a finger over magenta
edging the soft petals like texts
etched in a forgotten language.

I want Paeon, their namesake, to return
with tinctures, with cures
like those that healed, in Homer's songs,
the wounds of Hades and Ares.

Today I need an ancient god to tend my sister,
to send ravaging cells back
to whatever hell they came from.

Physician of gods, accompany her.
Place your hands on the gurney
that wheels her into the room of masks
and gowns, shields and practiced hands.

Though she does not know your name,
she knows your sign: buds that swell

and unlock each spring.
She has tasted the fragrance of your flower.
She knows their touch.

I THOUGHT THE CUP WAS EMPTY

for Elinor

Miss Blue's child drinks from the cup each morning.
Some day she will read Heidegger or Kant.
Today she fills her self up with the tangible world:

the jay's screen-door complaint,
a pale handkerchief pressed and folded for her pocket,
slim lines marking the margin in her notebook:
blue, blue, blue.

> I thought the cup was empty,
> but all it meant was I was ready
> to follow a thread
> and open the cabinet
> where the past was hidden.

Milk pours into her glass,
makes bubbles when she stirs it hard.
The clink of her spoon—
blue notes and blue melodies.

> I thought the cup was empty,
> but it was filled with sorrow.
> It held joy as well.
> It must have.

I thought the cup was empty.
I was wrong.

WHAT I WANTED THIS MORNING

That shining. That drift

and drop. That slim
convulsion.

That mingle. That edge
and delineation.

I wanted to know you
and for that
I had to
leave you.

Had to become torn
branch.

Cast forth
broken.

The solitary.

I had to be the bolt
unthreaded

and the wrench
at rest.

ELEVEN

for Sam

Not an even number, even though
it holds all that is needed
for even. Even holds them
in the correct order.

But what to do with that
miniature snail, the extra *e*?
What to do with *l*,
a lamppost without a lamp,
flagpole with no flag?

Even when inscribed in an
upward/downward loop,
l builds a wall.
Ask a friend to give
you a boost. Peek over,
then scramble to the tippy top
and dive into the valley of *v*
where an invisible river flows.

Wade across. Climb out.
Hike toward the mound of *n*,
not an actual end,
but a resting place.

Take a breath,
many breaths, before
even glancing at 12,
that place of dig and delve,
distant, but looming.

Hold onto 11 as long as you can,
11, where odd ones are welcome.
11, that haven where every
odd inclination finds heaven,
home.

MAYBE REVERENCE

At seventeen I wanted beauty, not a dagger.
I believed in dreams chastened by the real.
Wanted earth beneath my feet, not air.

I wanted the minor chord,
the dark side of the moon.
How I wanted.

Now we invent new catastrophes.
Dictionaries filled with blur.
Chartreuse cries, no occasion.

Old man James passes by in his gray coat.
We aren't sure we like him anyway—
now jovial, now bitter as nails.

We're into the malleable.
Click, click, clack. The hardware.
Not the oil in the machine.

From under the floorboards,
a snake insinuates its length
into the room, circles my wrist.

Cool scales, deliberate calm.
Maybe reverence will save me.

LUMINOUS

with a line from Kyle Dargan

Maybe, like the Easter lily, you will not choose
to keep your trumpet of light and scent
secreted in your own arms, sturdy as they are.

You will radiate incandescent
star power, heat along with light.
No slap of wind will snuff you out.

Like certain plankton, like fireflies,
you will float or flit, sending messages
kindled by circumstance and need.

You will alight on a dry reed
like this morning's first red-winged blackbird,
its chevron patches glinting like sparks.

The sky's mother-of-god blue
will shine with your eyes.
Maybe you will be self-luminous

lighting up the sanctuary of the ordinary,
your urge to reveal greater
than your need to conceal,

the padlock and chains binding your heart
Houdini-ed: all the horses of the sea galloping
just beyond your window.

IMPERVIOUS

imagine your heart is just a ball you learned to dribble up
and down the length of your driveway back home.
—BRIONNE JANAE

or a pinball, which, with a tug and release,
you send rolling up the incline, glancing off
clown faces, pressing levers, escaping
the little cliffs and declivities
crafted to snag it. Imagine
the aria of bells and clangs
each time you pull the knob or knock
against the sides of the machine.

Your heart, impervious to slap and jangle,
shining and beautiful, with only one chamber,
no doors or windows, no separate rooms
for aches or specters to hide, subject
only to the whims of your own hands.
And to gravity, to chance.

"Are you in pain?" yet another nurse, doc, case advisor
asks my sister with cancer lodged in her chest.
"Heart pain. We're both in heart pain."
One more explication of their grief.

Some days the most profound thing you do
is lift a dead animal from the asphalt

and place it in the grass. Today, a dark calico
already stiffening, its blood still scarlet.

Forgive the errant driver,
forgive the cat running careless
across the road. Just another matter
for your sturdy heart,
that steel warrior still in play.

EPISTEMOLOGY II

The work of the imagination is to turn knowns into unknowns.
—RICHARD HUGO

You know you will die, as surely
as did the cardinal your cat left on the stoop.
You know the names of trees and wildflowers.
You know cold will loosen starch and hot, melt sugar.

You remember the diatom's symmetry and forget the photon's
    speed.
You wish you knew the meaning of the dragon tattoo
on your son's left shoulder and what is hidden behind his eyes.

We turn knowns into unknowns
to see them as on the first day,
when they were urgent as tsunami warning,
urgent as tongue touching tongue.

Stone into cave, and cave into the primal base of the brain.
Turn wind into muse and rain into amber,
trapping beetle and mite.

We turn unknowns into maybes: we parse and parse
her final letter, his online manifesto, hoping to divine
the reason she took her life, the reason he shot
into the crowd, as though knowing will stay the next hand,
quench the inferno while yet a spark.

AFTER LIFE

Wouldn't it be a surprise, she thought,
to die and not be truly gone,
but to survive in some manner
on what her cousin referred to
as "the spiritual plane."

It seemed presumptuous
to be sure about absolute oblivion:
not quite like never having ever been,
another state of mind and body
she found alternatingly troubling
and comforting.

Both like and unlike the pliable body
of the garter snake lying in a soft curve
on the footpath by the detention basin
where red-wings made their claim.
She held the snake, let its
sleek length slip through her fingers
before placing it in shade under a bush.
Its black bead eyes were still open.
Not one part of its body seemed fraught.

Perhaps a person, too, might pass
from this side to the other
without being marked. She guessed
the going would be easy, though what precedes

be pain or violence. If there were continuation,
wouldn't she be ashamed to leave
so much work undone?

She couldn't fathom hell, not the fabled kind.
Of what use could that be to any god?
All those fires to tend and the job of extinction
never accomplished. Surely a god would prefer
to be opening the five petals on each apple blossom
or allowing a girl tend the hunger of her sex.

It was Easter and talk about resurrection
woke an old ache in her mind.
She tried to imagine taking her mother's hand
the way she almost never had,
asking her father questions
she had never framed,
holding Ellen's shoulders,
not letting go.

TRUE BLUE AND FALSE BLUE AND BLUE IN-BETWEEN

In sleep, I reach for the girl who has not yet discerned
her pink labia or tendered her own un-budded breasts,
the girl who loves cats and singing.
When she is found chained to the bed,
those next door will claim they know nothing,
but my dream draws near to her center,
widens to touch her fingertips, her toes.
The dream yearns for a boat she can row
toward another shore.

Awake, I tell you my brain is filled with cotton.
Weave it, you say. The finest gauze for her wound,
dimity to curtain her windows, a spread of chintz
sprinkled with purple violets.
Weave sateen to ease her pain.

Let her look in the mirror and tell herself, *tonight*,
then fold the three dresses of fairy tale so tight
they snug into a walnut shell: one golden,
one silver, one that glints like a star.
"There," she will say, and tuck the walnut into her pocket,
pull on her boots, her hat, her coat with the crimson hood,
and let herself out into the night.

Perhaps she will die,
holding in her fist a thought so strange,

death being the country of the old or the sick, of the boy
who no longer sat at his desk in the row by the window,
the boy with hair like straw.

For now, she will keep walking, and I,
weaving her story out of vapor and forgetting, will wait
while the night fills with snow.

TELL ME, WHOM DO YOU LOVE?

Though your wife will be troubled
if you tell her, it's much better
to love the dog.
The dog does not care if you forget
the turn that takes both of you
back to your door, is not
alarmed when you spoon soup
into your shirt pocket, will never
fasten a monitor around your wrist
and set out your clothes.
The dog races to the window
to bark at nothing
then returns to your side
and forgets, like you.
Better to love the dog.

When the dog's time comes,
you will press her head to your chest
as the needle finds the vein.
You will stroke her flank
and slip her soft ears through your fingers.
You will wait for her breathing to stop.
Carefully, you will make out the check
and in the memo line write,
"Rosie, good-bye," before you take the receipt
and go out to the car. Perhaps you will
lean your head against the steering wheel

and let your weeping fog the windshield.
Then, not burdened by stories of heaven or hell,
you will drive.

MEMORIAL DAY

I

Cormorants crowd the pier.
Some lift heads skyward. Others huddle.
This mumbling congregation
is safer than the fifth-graders I will visit tomorrow,
twenty children ready to be sprung for summer.

Surely they are safer than any two women
chatting in front of a church, safer than a surgeon
whose patient blames the doc for his pain,
safer than the platter-sized snapper
crossing the nearby road
on the way to dig into sand and lay her eggs.

One bird lifts from its fellows
and skims the wind-creased surface,
touches downs and dives.
I count: 20, 30, nearly 40 seconds
before it surfaces.
How many bullets can pass through the barrel
of a semi-automatic rifle in 40 seconds?

II

When you are dead, a five-year-old tells me,
you don't get undead. Innocent
of zombies and werewolves,
she is talking about the boy

whose gravestone has cut short
the shortcut we are taking
back to our car from the parade.

A fleet of tiny toy trucks at the stone's base
has caught her attention.
She demands I read everything
engraved on the stone for Henry,
who was born in the spring of one year
and died during summer just two years later.

It's a memory stone, she says, touching
the small tan one that rests on the granite.
And that's his picture. Love doesn't end, she adds.
She is five.

SILK

Just try to forget the word silk, and you'll be reminded. . . .
—INGER CHRISTENSEN

of the empire-waist dress you made for that high school dance.
The dance all wrong—the date, the weather, tears in the girls'
restroom, teachers gossiping at the door; but the *dress*: next-to-
perfect: blue and green jewel-tone silk wanting to be slipped
through fingers, yielding to scissors, pins, presser foot and the
finest needle you could thread. A dress without weight, ready
to lift, turn, swirl. Even the ribbon you slipped through the
side seam loops —so soft you could barely bear to pull taut
the bow.

Try to forget the word and you will think of every silken cliché
that became a cliché because it was befitting: baby's cheek,
friable skin of an old man's forearm, corn silk, silky dream,
spider silk, milk like silk, silken voice in the passage where the
soprano laments her lost love.

You will be reminded of spices and tales of dragons, of camels
carrying packs from China to Samarkand, of desert nights and
the way the camels could smell an oasis long before the first
green crested the horizon.

Try to forget and you will think of scarves and scars that age
into whiteness, of custard stirred slowly over a low, low flame.

Think of honey and soapstone carvings, of lace-edged handker-
chiefs and Sunday petticoats.

Conjure up every other fabric you have worn with pleasure:
wide-wale corduroy, fine-gauge linen, velvet and velveteen,
faded calico, Liberty lawn, stonewashed denim; even your
father-in-law's old acrylic sweater, the softest memory you have
of him.

Try to forget the word *silk,* and you will be reminded of the
times you had nothing but your flannel nightgown and wind
racketing at the window, your parents asleep behind a closed
door and light so far away.

SMELL OF IRON

for my father

Dust on the rafters,
a pigeon's elegant crop and noisy wings,
light through a high barn window.

Corncrib tight with dry ears
and winter coming on strong.
Skim ice topping the barrel, morning
frozen like children playing statues.

Smell of iron, soft-grained pine:
could these retrieve you?

All of my answers come from a dream,
the questions as well.

Here in this world, where dilemma resides,
fifteen deer, maybe twenty,
lie cattle-like among trees
browsed clear of undergrowth.

Where will the next forest come from?
"Just write one," a child advises. "Do it!"
And so I try,

stitching these remnants you left me,
searching the Whatnot Shop once more,
painting the rickety bookshelf pale blue sky.

TEAL SWEATER

All week I have been trying to remember the set
of my father's shoulders, the particular way
your father walked, his forward tilt and nod.
Some things retreat and some remain.

Some really are indestructible or nearly so,
like the Orlon V-neck sweater your father once wore,
the one I kept when we cleared out your parents' house.
That probably-ugly 100% soft sweater I've put on again,

pulling its comfort over my just-washed hair,
so I can wear it all day, thinking of how
my own father's soul might just now be continuing
its tenuous existence in the gray den of a cloud

or the slow movement of a Beethoven string quartet.
I'm thinking of your father and mother
and how we rarely speak of them,
except to further confound their difficult lives.

The sweater was made in the USA;
that would have made our fathers happy.
Over 20 years ago, yours must have bought it
at Penney's or Kaufmann's, driving out

to the Century III Mall in the Chevy Caprice,
stopping to flirt with the girl at the register

at Bress's or Three Daughters' Grocery,
leaving your mother at home, procrastinating

over a second cup of coffee, daunted by the prospect
of dressing for the day. So distant from when
she took the bus downtown in proper suit and hat.
Before she gave up her job, married for love.

Some things disappear before you have a chance
to take them into your arms or your mind.
Some as distinct as the image of a snowflake
captured by a photomicroscope, others fluid as mist.

Most stones sink, but others—unaccountably—float.
A raft of feathers, a concrete boat.

SACRED

Easy to mix up with scarred
or scared. Something akin to
terror both the known
and unknown engender.

Even if you seek it, you find it hard
to let yourself be lifted or lowered,
to come that close to peace or peril,
your hair yanked by the blast

or parted and quietly braided
as you perch on the green chair
in your grandmother's kitchen,
her gnarled fingers felt, but not seen.

You stare at the calendar picture
of men in pastel robes standing in dazzle
by a pool of water, ringed by white columns.
It's a place unlike any you've seen
on an ordinary day.

You don't want to go there,
but you like the calm face
of the man who leans over the pool.

He reaches a hand
to one coming up out of the water,

brown beard dripping, eyes startled like those
of a bird who did not know what might happen,
but left the branch and fluttered its wings.

ENTHUSIASMUS

Alleluia calls from blue
as morning glory surges
over chain-link

but I drive on, pushed by traffic,
pulled by promise;
use one hand to find a pencil,
an old envelope, begin
to scribble this blue sound.

Her face filled with falling in love,
my friend wears the complexities
of marriage, real estate, parenting
as lightly as the shoulder pads
tucked inside her coral blouse.

Below each earlobe
swings a miniature mobile:
porcupine quills shimmer
from a cloud of jade.

Our talk plunges, leaps.
We can't keep on any subject,
baffle the waitress with questions.
No means *no,*
she seems to sigh.

But we know
other: *no* turned *yes.*
Light sung blue
in a thousand morning-glory throats.

COURTING SLEEP WITH THICH NHAT HANH

Open the familiar volume
as though it were
a bible and you the one seeking a text
for the day ahead or for ruminating
on the day behind.

Turn a page. Stitch or glue a wound
toward healing.
Let all severing be over.

A-men, ah-women, ah-human,
poor creature that you are,
not gifted with scent skill like dog
or agility like squirrel, elasticity
and squirm like worm,

or the gift of metamorphosis
like monarch, swallowtail, checkerspot,
or patience and flight like heron and hawk,
or longevity like the oaks: mossy cup,
burr, chinkapin, white;

or modesty like
the soft-threaded grass under maples
in front of grandmother's house,
yielding and kind to bare feet.

Each summer, there it was
for running and rolling,
or collapsing face up
to look through the branches, higher
than we could imagine.

Close the book.
Go there.

AT 4:00 A.M.

the unexamined life is
        an unruffled lake in which I float,
                and float and float

letting its unobservable current take me
        to the fair island Langston promised,
                close enough to be seen,

turning my mind from forsaking
        my past or seeking my future,
                toward the coming hour

in which I might attend to the lily,
        its orange stars blooming
                on a sturdy stem,

in which I might meet the burned girl,
        and learn her pain,
                take it with me

as I live in my own body,
        this working body
                that does what it can.

Yesterday, in the garden,
        a snake held a bird's wing in its mouth
                and didn't let go.

In the swallows' nest,
        the first brood jostled,
                all open mouth and squeal.

Light comes,
        deep inner light,
                a stubborn flicker.

        Let that be enough.

EPILOGUE

POEM ENDING WITH A LINE
BY E. E. CUMMINGS

Words are the worms,
the worms in the gut,

the ache in the chest,
the gout in the toe

towing the line,
the current so swift.

Worms are the words,
shed with the shit.

Words are the worms
impaled on the hook

cast into stream
where hungers hang.

They echo in hollows,
in hallows and hills.

worms are the words but joy's the voice

Acknowledgments

This book owes more than one debt of gratitude:
    to the many poets in my life whose own work and whose mea-
    sured responses to my nascent poems have kept me trying to
    shape experience into something that might speak to others

    to the poets who have gone before me, and those much younger
    than I, whose words have opened doors for me

    to Ethel Rackin who helped me refine and shape the book

    and to Ellen Foos, editor and publisher whose meticulous care
    is evident in the beauty of the volumes lucky enough to come to
    being through her work

    to my husband Paul and wise children Chelsea and Jesse for
    their confidence

    to time itself which both mars and burnishes

Kestrel: A Journal of Literature and Art: "Luminous," "A Small
God," "On the Day of the First Memorial Service for George
Floyd"

American War Against Itself, Moonstone Arts Center: "A Bullet with
Your Name on It"

US1 Worksheets: "Bluebeard's Boots," "On Assignment at the Home
for Disturbed Children: Poland, 1948," "Maybe Reverence"

Stillwater Review: "Prayer"

Schuylkill Valley Journal: "Little Goddess," "The Sky," "Poem with
the Teensy Tattoo," "Place Unknown/Known"

Poetry Ink: "Tongue"

River Heron Review: "Another Letter to Nâzim"

Poems for the Writing: Prompts for Poets: "It Was January"

"Of   of the: with lines from Sappho" was displayed in The Writers Room at Drexel University with by a painting by Emma Ward.

About the Author

Luray Gross grew up on a Pennsylvania dairy farm in a household full of music and books. Reading poetry out loud helped her survive the tumult of adolescence, and poetry has helped keep her sane ever since. She has recently been writing poems in response to the work of other writers and to the events of the day. She is the author of four collections of poetry, most recently *Lift*, also by Ragged Sky Press. A Dodge poet and faculty member of Murphy Writing of Stockton University, she was awarded a Fellowship in Poetry by the New Jersey State Council on the Arts and named one of their Distinguished Teaching Artists. She was the 2002 Poet Laureate of Bucks County (PA) and resident faculty at the Frost Place Festival and Conference on Poetry. A storyteller as well as a poet, she has worked with thousands of students of all ages during her many years as a Teaching Artist. She now lives with her husband and numerous pets only a few miles from her childhood home.